Leichte PANZERS in Action

created by Uwe Feist
captions by Mike Dario

squadron/signal publications

COPYRIGHT © 1974 by SQUADRON/SIGNAL PUBLICATIONS, INC.

NO PART OF THIS BOOK MAY BE REPRODUCED IN ANY FORM WITHOUT WRITTEN PERMISSION FROM THE PUBLISHER.
3461 E. TEN MILE ROAD, WARREN, MICHIGAN 48091

PHOTO CREDITS:

Bundesarchiv Koblenz
Walter J. Spielberger
Uwe Feist Archive
Squadron/Signal Archive
James Crow
Hans Zarbst
Norm E. Harms Archive
Otto Meyer

Panzerkampfwagen I Ausf. A

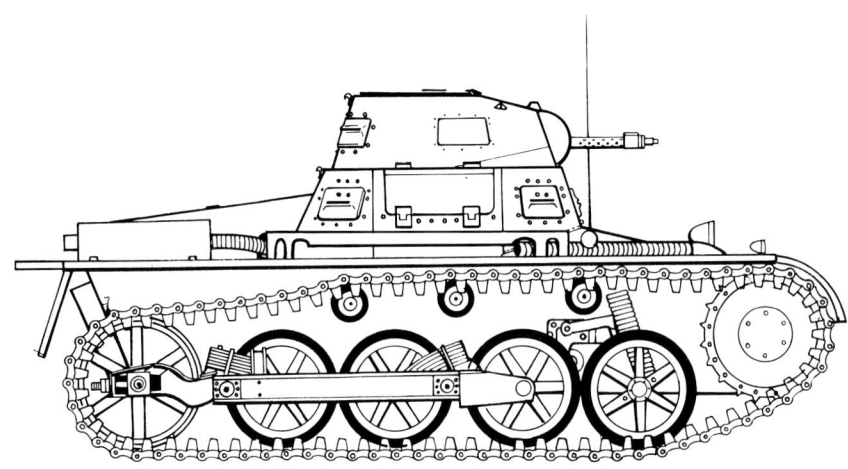

After the First World War the German military was fully aware that the restrictions of the Treaty of Versailles would in one way or another have to be violated in order to preserve and protect the Army and Germany's military society. The testing and development of equipment and munitions, banned under provisions of the Treaty of Versailles, began shortly after 1920 under a cloak of secrecy and continued until well into the 1930's even after Hitler became Chancellor.

As the design and development of armored vehicles moved slowly through the decade of the 1920's, long range plans and specifications for the vehicles that would ultimately become the backbone of the Wehrmacht's **Panzertruppe** were finalized. General Lutz, commander of the German motorized corps, had been told by the **Heereswaffenamt** (ordnance office), that development of the final vehicles would take between five and seven years, consequently interim types would have to be developed in the meantime. These interim vehicles were to be used for training the Panzertruppen who would later field Germany's main combat tanks, the Panzers III and IV.

In 1933, the Heereswaffenamt opened contracts for the construction of a series of armored vehicles between four and seven tons in weight. Bids were returned by Krupp of Essen, Henschel in Kassel, Daimler-Benz in Berlin and Maschinenfabrik Augsburg-Nürnberg (MAN) in Nürnberg. All companies submitted prototype vehicles that were quite similar to each other, and Krupp's was selected. Quantity production of the vehicles began in mid-1934 under the designation of Panzerkampfwagen IA (Sd.Kfz. 101).

These vehicles weighed 5.4 tons with combat loads. The PzKpfw. IA measured 13'3" in length, height from ground to top of turret was only 5'9", and its overall width was 6 ft. 9 in. Powered by a Krupp

A fully armed *Panzer IA* crawls slowly up a steep embankment during an exercise. Although unconfirmed, it is believed that the red and white checkerboard stripe around the top of the turret is an indicator that the vehicle is being used by student drivers during qualifications on their final driving examinations.

The *Panzer IA's* idler wheel was on ground level, this was changed on the later Panzer IB.

"Boxer" M305 air-cooled engine, a horizontally opposed four-cylinder design, displacing 211 cubic inches and producing 60 horsepower at 2500 rpm. The transmission was a standard crash-box type with five forward and one reverse gear.

The Sd.Kfz. 101 had an internal fuel capacity of 38 gallons, a maximum speed of 23 mph, and a tactical range of 91 miles. It could climb a 58% grade, negotiate vertical obstacles of up to 14" in height, cross trenches of 55" in width and ford streams of up to 23". Ground pressure was fair at 5.7 pounds per square inch and the power to weight ratio with the "Boxer" engine was a rather low 11.1 horsepower per ton.

The Panzerkampfwagen IA was crewed by only two men; one serving as driver and the other performing the duties of vehicle commander, radioman and machine-gunner. Main armament was a pair of rifle caliber machine guns mounted side-by-side in the turret with an effective range of 300 yards; the shot patterns were adjusted to converge at this range. A total of 3125 rounds of ammunition was carried on board the vehicle.

Although the Sd.Kfz. 101 was built primarily as a training vehicle, it saw combat action during the Spanish Civil War between 1937 and 1939. Over 1500 of these vehicles took part in the Polish Campaign, and in steadily dwindling numbers they participated in the invasion of the Low Countries, Norway, Africa, France, Greece, the Balkans, and even a few were used during the opening months of the invasion of the Soviet Union.

The Panzerkampfwagen IA was not an exceptionally good combat vehicle, suffering from lack of power, inadequate armament, and thin armor. She did, nevertheless, accomplish her primary mission by training thousands of new Panzer crews to drive track-laying vehicles and introduced her many charges to the complexities of vehicle crew coordination in both individual and unit combat tactics.

While narrow the *Panzer IA* track had a fair ground pressure of 5.7 pounds per square inch, it was however an extremely maneuverable vehicle.

Panzerkampfwagen I Ausf. A
(Sd.Kfz. 101)

TECHNICAL DATA

Manufacturer	Henschel, MAN
Production Year	1934 - 1936
No. Built	477 vehicles
Crew	2 men
Weight	5.4 tons (5400 kg)
Length	13'3"
Width	6'9"
Height	5'8"
Engine	4 cyl. air cooled Krupp M 305 (Boxer)
Horsepower	60 BHP/2500 r.p.m.
Transmission	5 forward, 1 reverse
Brake steering	2. -4. syncronised
Track width	280 mm
Clearance	295 mm
Armor	13 mm / 7 mm
Armament	2 x 7.92 mm MG
Ammunition	3125 rounds
Fuel	2 tanks 72 ltr. ea.
	144 ltr. (appr. 38 Imp. gal.) stored in the engine compartment
Consumption	Road 70 ltr., cross country 100
Range	Road 200 km. cross country 140 km.
Top speed	37 km/h (23 m.p.h.)

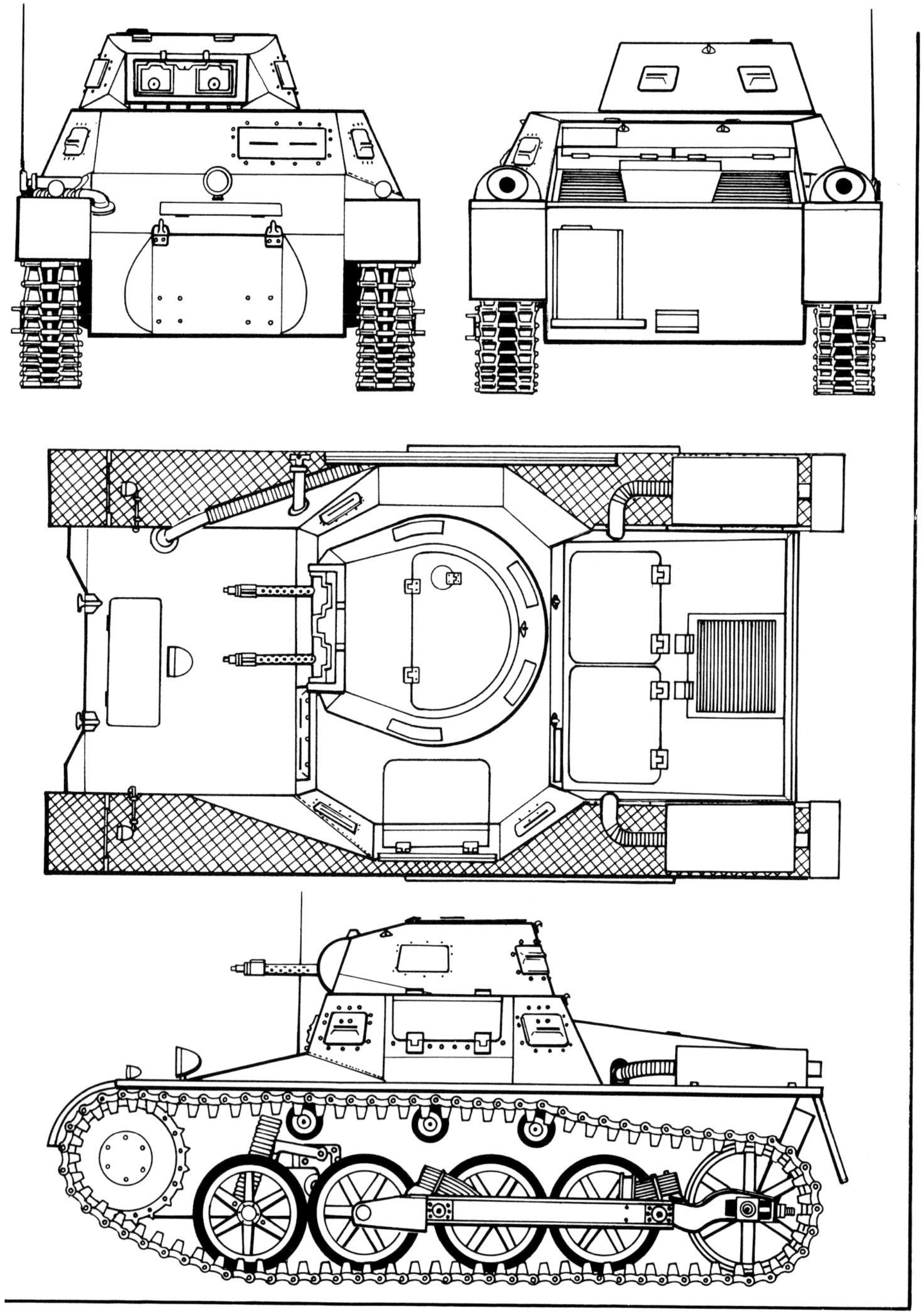

A show of armored strength. *Panzer IB's* form up on "Unter den Linden" in front of the Brandenburg Gate bedecked with Nazi banners. This photograph was taken in 1935 and most of the vehicles shown here ultimately went to Spain as part of the "Legion Condor" where they received their "baptism under fire."

(Below left) Tag der Wehrmacht (Day of the Army) is shown in a still from one of the impressive scenes of Riefenstahl's propaganda film, "Triumph des Willens" (triumph of the willpower). The film was a documentary of the growth of Germany behind the leadership of the Nazi party and was full of formal military reviews and NSDAP celebrations such as the one seen here with Pz. IA vehicles passing in review in Nürnberg during an army celebration.

A platoon of *Panzer IA* vehicles dressed to the right passes the camera. The vehicle leading the platoon is the so called "Kleiner Panzerbefehlswagen" (small command vehicle), a modification of the Panzer I chassis that included a rigid built-up superstructure without a turret. From these vehicles, tactical unit commanders could provide a valuable radio communication and control link between the battalion and platoons.

"Feuerschlag" all guns of the Panzer I and Panzer II as well as the KwK's of the Panzer III's are firing at a signal given over the radio. Blanks are used for this exercise and as indicated by the smoke, thousands of rounds are released in seconds; most impressive for the crowd and visiting military personnel from foreign armies.

PANZERTRUPPE STANDER

Panzer I Ausf. A with the MG turret at one o'clock operates as an infantry support weapon during early field exercises to adjust both infantry and cavalry to the presence of armoured vehicles. In order to weld these three basically dissimilar elements into a fighting unit many such joint exercises were held.

The two-man crews of these *Panzer IA's* stand before their vehicles during an inspection. The company commander can be seen at the right of the photograph wearing a white shirt and necktie along with a Sam Browne belt. Note the open turret hatches of the vehicles and the large open visors used by the drivers.

A *Panzer I* unit rests during a pause in maneuvers. The crewmembers of these armored vehicles wear the standard Panzer black uniforms featuring a double breasted jacket decorated with salmon pink piping around the epaulets, collar and lapels. The numeral "3" on the epaulets indicates the 3rd Panzer Regiment. The black berets were worn over a leather helmet that protected the crewmembers from injuring their head while in the vehicle. When not in the vehicles, the beret was worn without the leather protective under-helmet.

Mounting and dismounting their vehicle was an exercise practiced by the Panzer crews over and over again. A former tank driver who went through six years of action told this writer that their body was bruised all over after a day of this "nonsense". However, he soon appreciated the training he had gone through, when altogether five tanks were shot out from under him and only an expedient departure from the burning vehicle saved his life.

A formation of *Panzer IA's* with playing card maneuver markings on the right rear mud guard. Clearly seen is the early panzer multi-colored camouflage scheme of grey, brown, and green. The four cylinder air-cooled Krupp M305 engine was housed in the rear of the vehicle and protected by 13mm armor plates.

Typical camouflage scheme

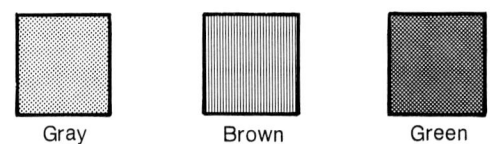

Gray   Brown   Green

Panzer IA's negotiate a deep anti-tank trench during maneuvers. These vehicles also bear the brown, green and grey camouflage scheme as well as a modified arrowhead insignia painted on the rear of the turrets; a marking used only in maneuvers. Although rather underpowered, these vehicles were still capable of negotiating rough terrain.

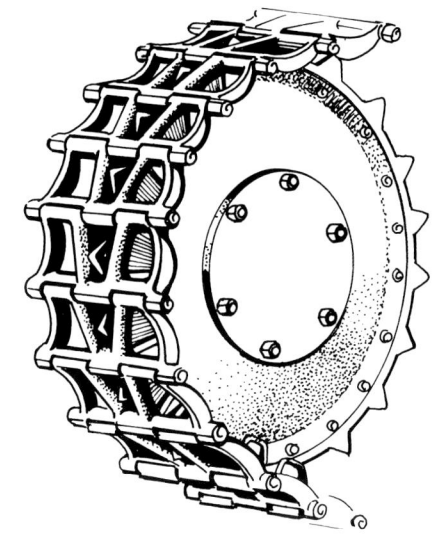

Drive sprocket of Panzer I

A *Panzer IA* rolls out of heavy brush to cross an open meadow during Reichswehr maneuvers in Lünenburger, as a machine gun team uses the tank for cover. The gun carried by the machine gunners is a World War One vintage Spandau Model 08/15. A total of 477 Panzer IA's left the production line between 1934 and 1936.

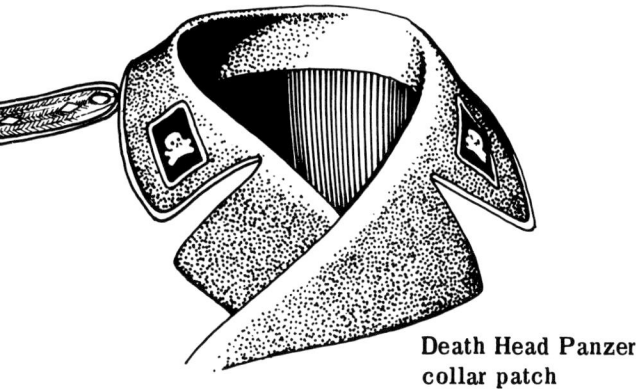

Death Head Panzer collar patch

Bogged down. Bearing the mud, grass and hay indicative of the crew's attempt to free the vehicle from the sticky mud, this Panzer IA awaits the powerful winch of a recovery vehicle. This scene was repeated time and again in Spain and Poland due to the inability of the Pz.Kpfw. IA's engine to get itself out of trouble.

September 1934, the first tanks are moving into their new barracks (Kasernen).

(Below left) Practiced only for propaganda purposes, a *Pz. IA* is smashing through a freshly built brick wall. All regulations advise against using the tank as a bulldozer since falling debris and dust could seriously clog up the air intake, ventilation, visors, also block the turret and escape hatches and foul up the MG and/or KwK gun.

A line-up of *Panzer IA's* at rest in a motor park. All of these armored fighting vehicles have been disarmed by removal of the twin MG 13 7.92mm machine guns from their turrets. It was a common practice to remove all radio equipment and weapons from armored vehicles and store them indoors during peacetime because of the high humidity inside the vehicles when they were "buttoned up".

1 September 1939

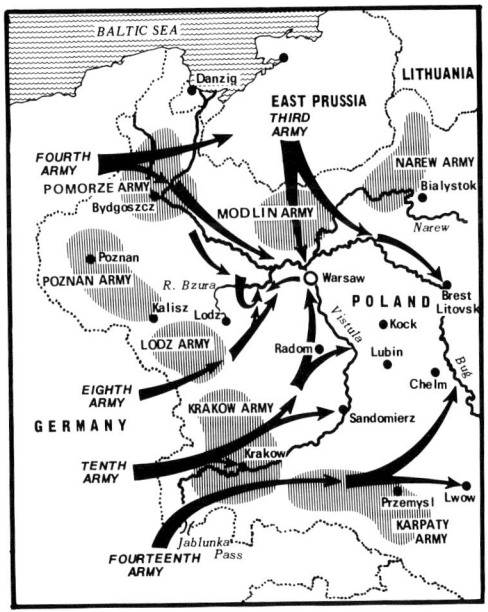

When the Wehrmacht crossed the Frontier and moved into Poland at 0445 on 1 September 1939 a great number of the armored vehicles on first line strength were the *Panzer IA's* sporting thin armor and only machine guns as their offensive weapons as can be seen with these Panzer IA's during the opening stages of the spearhead into Poland.

PANZERSCHUTZMUTZE

Panzer IA's and *Panzer IB's* could not absorb much damage. Small arms fire and splinters would not stop the light tank, however, mines and antitank rifles were often fatal. This Pz. IA rests abandoned on the road after being hit by antitank rifle fire. The turret vision slits are blown open by an internal explosion.

Panzerkampfwagen I Ausf. B

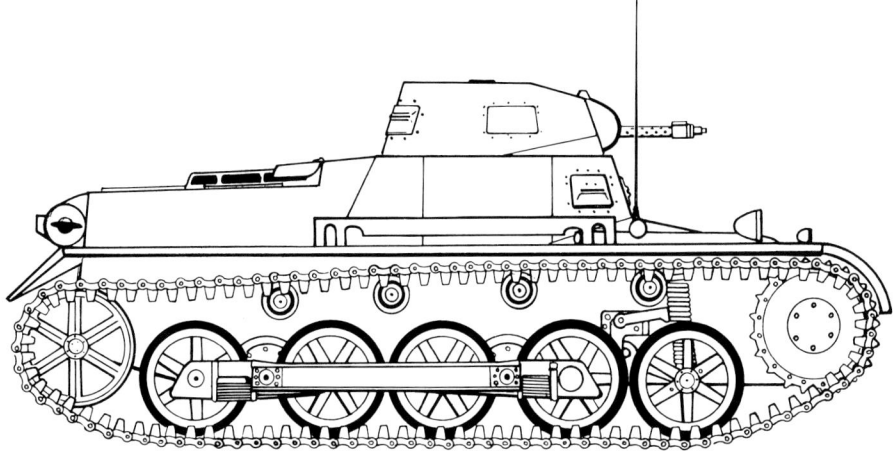

Since the Krupp M305 air-cooled engine of the Panzerkampfwagen IA was not as powerful as was desired, plans were made to provide a new power plant for the vehicle. The engine was to be a six-cylinder water-cooled version, but major changes to the chassis would be required before the engine could be fitted. The engine, designated Maybach NL38TR, displaced 231 cubic inches and was much larger than the "Boxer". At 3000 rpm, the engine produced 100 horsepower and was attached to the transmission originally installed in the earlier version of the Panzer I.

Placement of the engine required an extension of the engine compartment and the corresponding increase in weight created additional problems. The solution to the added weight problem (now 5.8 tons) was to add a fifth set of bogie wheels to the running gear to equalize the load. The rear idler wheels were moved from their ground level positions to a horizontal position so that the same length of track would maintain contact with the ground.

The **Panzerkampfwagen IB's** overall length was increased to 14'8½", but the height and width of the vehicle remained the same as those of its little brother. Internal fuel capacity remained at 38 gallons, but since the Maybach engine used more fuel than the "Boxer" tactical range was decreased to 87 miles. The vehicle's greater weight affected the speed of the up-engined Panzer IB, increasing top speed to only 25 mph on good roads. Crew and armament remained unchanged over the Pz.Kpfw. IA, as were most of the major performance areas. Construction techniques and armor thicknesses were basically the same with little or no differences.

First produced in 1935, these vehicles served alongside the Pz.Kpfw. IA variants through all of the German army's campaigns up through the invasion of the Soviet Union. As larger and better tanks became available to the Panzertruppen, Panzer I's were slowly phased out of first line service and relegated to their original role of training vehicles. A large number of the vehicles were converted into special purpose vehicles and continued to serve with combat units in new roles.

The **Panzerkampfwagen IB** proved to be only a little better than the IA variant in combat situations, suffering the same disadvantages, disabilities and inadequacies. Even though the Panzer I's were totally inadequate as main battle tanks, these little two man vehicles formed the mainstay of the German armored formations from their introduction in 1934 through the Blitzkrieg in France in 1940.

The Panzers found little resistance from the Polish armored vehicles. However, the enemy anti-tank weapons proved to be effective and the white crosses on the German tanks proved to be ideal aiming points easily visible and were soon changed.

Panzerkampfwagen I Ausf. B
(Sd.Kfz. 101)

TECHNICAL DATA

Manufacturer	Henschel, MAN, Wegmann
Production Year	1935 - 1939
No. Built	2000 vehicles
Crew	2 men
Weight	5.8 tons (5800 kg)
Length	14'8½"
Width	6'9"
Height	5'8"
Engine	Maybach NL 38 TR 6 cyl. water cooled
Horsepower	100 BHP/3000 r.p.m.
Transmission	5 forward, 1 reverse
Brake steering	2. -4. syncronised
Track width	280 mm
Clearance	295 mm
Armor	13 mm / 7 mm
Armament	2 x 7.92 mm MG
Ammunition	3125 rounds
Fuel	2 tanks 84 - 62 ltr. 146 ltr. (appr. 38 Imp. gal.) stored in the engine compartment
Consumption	Road 80 ltr., cross country 110
Range	Road 180 km., cross country 130 km.
Top speed	40 km/h (27 m.p.h.)

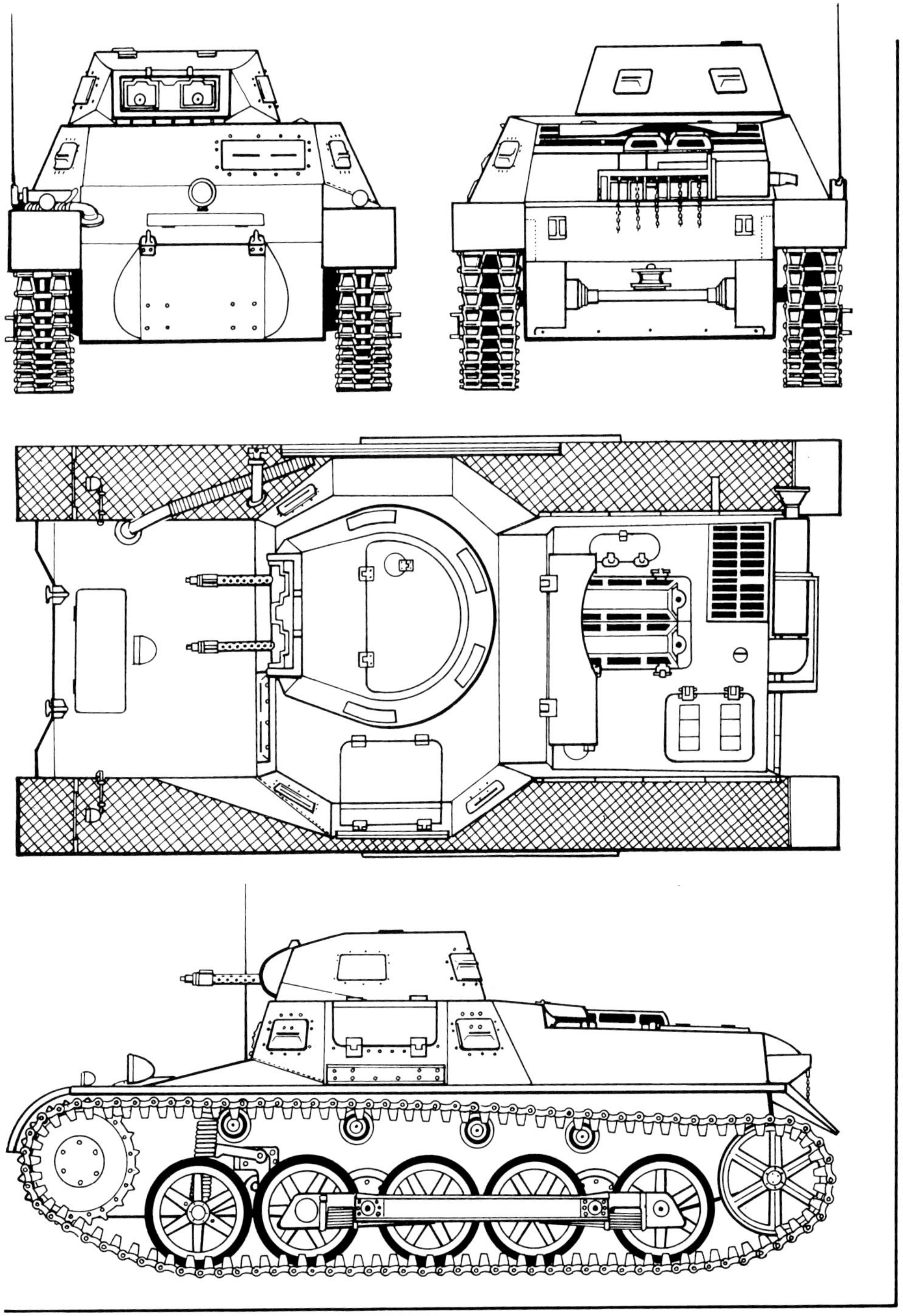

Panzer IB's move up to give support to a *Ladungsleger I,* a Panzer IB modified for use as an assault engineer vehicle for placing demolition charges against obstacles and enemy strongpoints. This photo was taken during the campaign in Holland, May, 1940.

(Above left) *Panzer I's* and *II's* in concealed positions along the Polish frontier prepare to move into action. The vehicle on the left is a Panzer I and the one on the right is an early version of the Panzer II light tank. The Pz. II's 20mm main gun can barely be seen protruding into the sunlight.

A *Panzer IB* follows a *Ladungsleger I.* The Ladungsleger I was capable of carrying a 160 pound demolition charge on its gantry and platform seen attached to the rear. This was only one of many uses found for the Panzer I chassis; a vehicle already obsolete as a combat tank prior to the beginning of the Second World War.

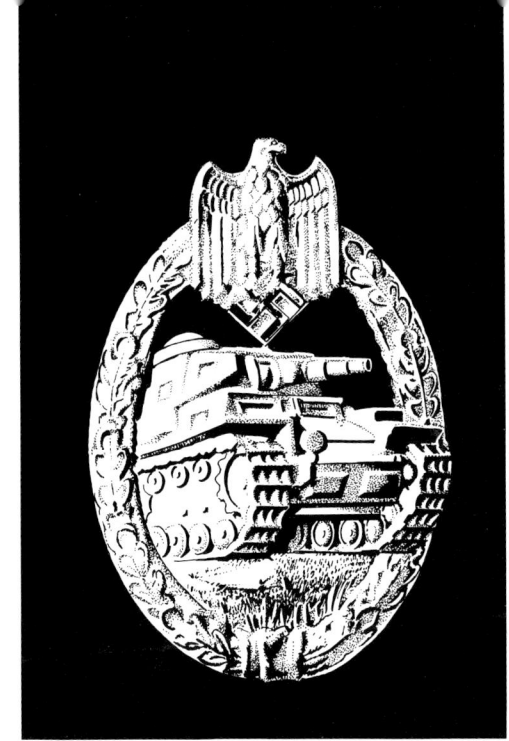

PANZER Assault Badge

Infantrymen gathered around a "Gulaschkanone", a mobile field kitchen, eat a hot meal while watching a column of *Panzer IB's* roll toward the front lines. Note the single muffler on the rear plate of the engine compartment of the rearmost tank — one of the recognition features of the Pz. IB.

Early style Balkenkreuze

A rare photograph of the deadly street-fighting that went on in the city of Warsaw during the last stages of the campaign in Poland. Infantrymen have taken cover behind this *Panzer IB* as this combined arms column approaches an enemy strong-point. A Panzer II can be seen behind the Panzer I in the foreground. Note that the whip antenna of the Panzer I has been broken and is laying across the vehicle's bowplate, disrupting communication. The white numerals 133 on the vehicle chassis is repeated in yellow on the turret, most unusual for this period.

Adolf Hitler and members of the general staff visit frontline troops after the victory in Poland. Hitler made this tour, visiting an extremely large number of units that had been in the fighting. It was common practice for him to talk with the troops and recount to them some of his experiences as a corporal during the First World War.

A *Panzer I* Ausführung B of 4. Panzer division is crossing the Dutch Border at the beginning of the Blitzkrieg of the low countries, May 1940. Of particular interest is the new style Balkenkreuze now in use and the red turret numbers outlined in white.

Middle style Balkenkreuze

A troop of *Panzer I's* including a *Panzerbefehlswagen* patrols the streets of Oslo, Norway after the German takeover in 1940. Only a token force of armored vehicles was sent to Norway, including a number of Panzer I's and a group of so-called "Neubaufahrzeuge," armored monstrosities built on the line of the British "Independent," with a number of turrets on each chassis.

A *Panzer 1B* leads a column of Czechoslovakian-built Panzer 38(t)'s across a grassy field in the north of France during the French Campaign of 1940. The Panzer 38(t) was issued to the German 7. and 8. Panzer Divisions during the spring of 1940.

(Below left) Engineers and civilians clear away a road block made largely of tree trunks so this *Panzer IB* can continue on its way. The photo was taken in May of 1940 and although the location is not confirmed, it may have been in Holland where the Dutch army threw up road blocks on virtually every major thoroughfare in that country.

A *Panzer IB* of the I.SS Panzer Division passes the staff vehicle of the division's commander during a review. "Sepp" Dietrich can be seen in the steel helmet standing next to Field-marshall Gerd Von Rundstedt reviewing the parade. June 1940.

Kleiner Panzer Befehlswagen I

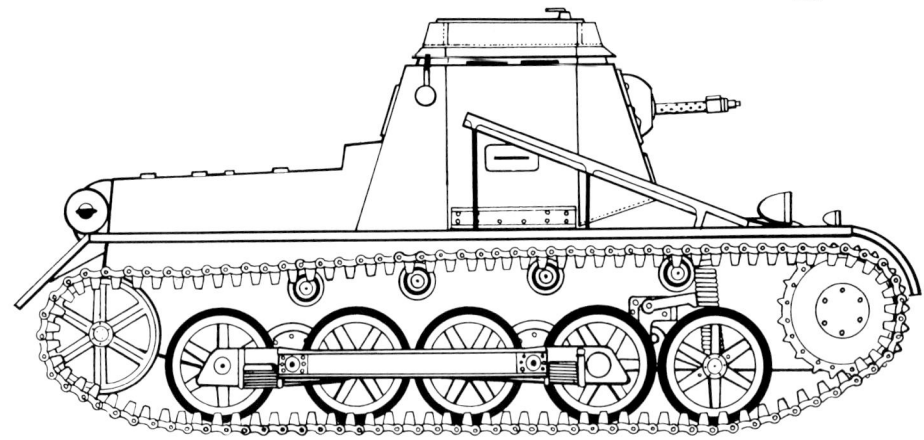

The **Sd.Kfz. 265 Kleiner Panzer Befehlswagen** was one of the major variants built on the chassis of the Panzerkampfwagen IA and IB. Over two hundred Panzer I chassis were converted as the basis for these special purpose vehicles, the major function of which was tactical command control. First developed in 1938, the vehicle carried

Performance remained the same as that of the Panzer I, but the armament was reduced to only a 7.92mm machine gun for defensive purposes. While the chassis armor was only slightly increased overall, the bowplate armor was thickened to 30mm and the driver's vision plate armor was increased to 34mm. Side armor was 23mm. The fighting compartment featured a frontplate of 34mm thickness, side armor was 30mm thick, and the rear plate was 16mm thick.

The crew of the vehicle alternated between two and three men; the third man only being responsible for communications if he were along. The German army placed much importance on these vehicles because they enabled a tactical commander to exercise direct communication and control over his unit. They first saw action in Poland in 1939 and remained in front line service until the end of 1941 when they were replaced by later more efficient types.

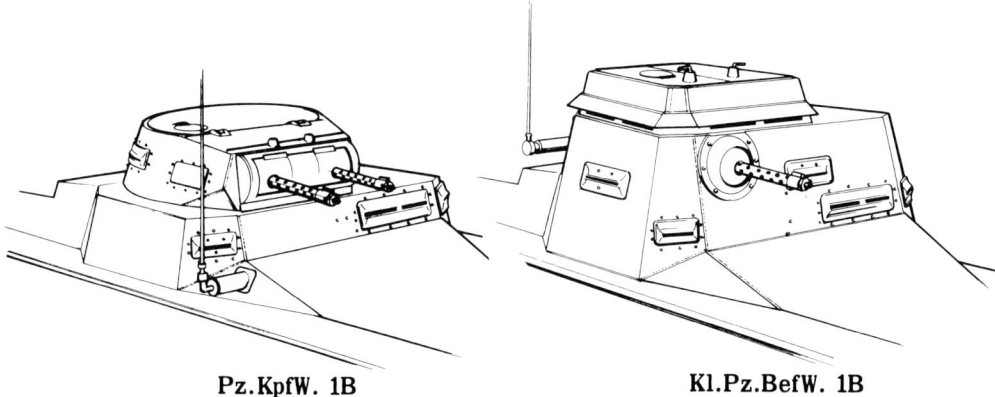

Pz.KpfW. 1B   Kl.Pz.BefW. 1B

two radio sets for communication with individual tanks in an armored unit, as well as with higher echelons of command, all the way to regimental level, if necessary. The major modification of the Panzer I was the removal of the turret and the adding on of a fighting compartment that raised the height of the vehicle to 6'4".

The *Panzerbefehlswagen I* during the campaign in Poland. This small command vehicle was the unit commander's variant of the Panzer IB featuring a fixed full-width superstructure that replaced the turret of the tank version. It carried extra radio equipment and was armed with one 7.92mm MG for self defense. The diagonal rack on the side of the vehicle closest to the camera is a protective rack for the two-meter radio antenna which is presently in its raised position.

This sergeant (Unteroffizier) uses a bullet to point to the place on the superstructure of his light command tank where it sustained a hit from a 7.92mm projectile, his other hand is resting on the antenna guard. These light command tanks were built on the chassis of the Panzer IB model, although a small number were built on the chassis of the Panzer IA version with fixed turrets were also used for this purpose.

(Above left) General der Panzer Heinz Guderian reviews the troops of a panzerkompanie during field exercises in Eastern Germany in October 1938. The vehicle leading the column is the *Sd.Kfz. 265* armored command vehicle armed with only a machine gun, that could be removed and used outside the tank while those following are the more powerful variant of the Panzer I, the *Ausführung B*.

A column of *Pz. IIc* tanks led by a *"Kleiner Panzerbefehlswagen I"*, form up to participate in a parade in Denmark, during the summer of 1940. The fourth vehicle in the column is a Panzerkampfwagen IB. Notice that the column leader is holding a standard convoy signal in his right hand. The signal he is giving is: "attention, command follows".

A motorcycle reconnaissance unit of 7. Panzer Division prepares to clear the roadway ahead for a Kl. Panzer Befehlswagen IB during the French campaign of 1940. This rarely photographed vehicle was fitted with a large frame antenna as well as a standard two-meter antenna which has been folded down in its rack.

Kleiner Panzer Befehlswagen I (Sd.Kfz. 265)

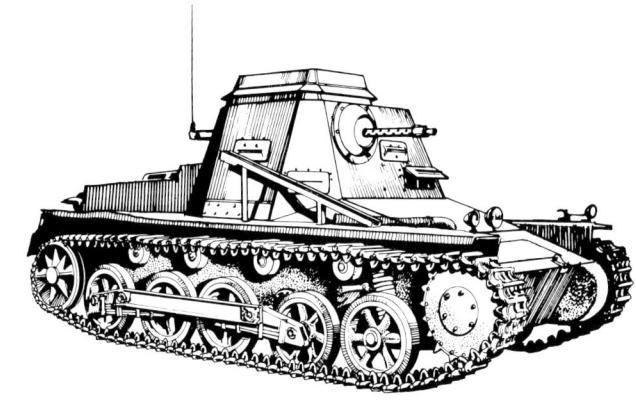

TECHNICAL DATA

Manufacturer	Daimler-Benz
Production Year	1936 - 1938
No. Built	150 vehicles
Crew	3 men
Weight	6 tons (6000 kg)
Length	14'8½"
Width	6'9"
Height	6'4"
Engine	6 cyl. Maybach NL 38 water cooled
Horsepower	100 hp/3000 r.p.m.
Transmission	5 forward, 1 reverse
Brake steering	2. -4. syncronised
Track width	280 mm
Clearance	295 mm
Armor	14 mm
Armament	1 x MG 34
Ammunition	900 rounds
Fuel	2 tanks 84-62 ltr. 146 ltr. (appr. 388 Imp. gal.) stored in the engine compartment
Consumption	Road 80 ltr., cross country 110
Range	Road 180 km, cross country 130 km.
Top speed	40 km/h (27 m.p.h.)

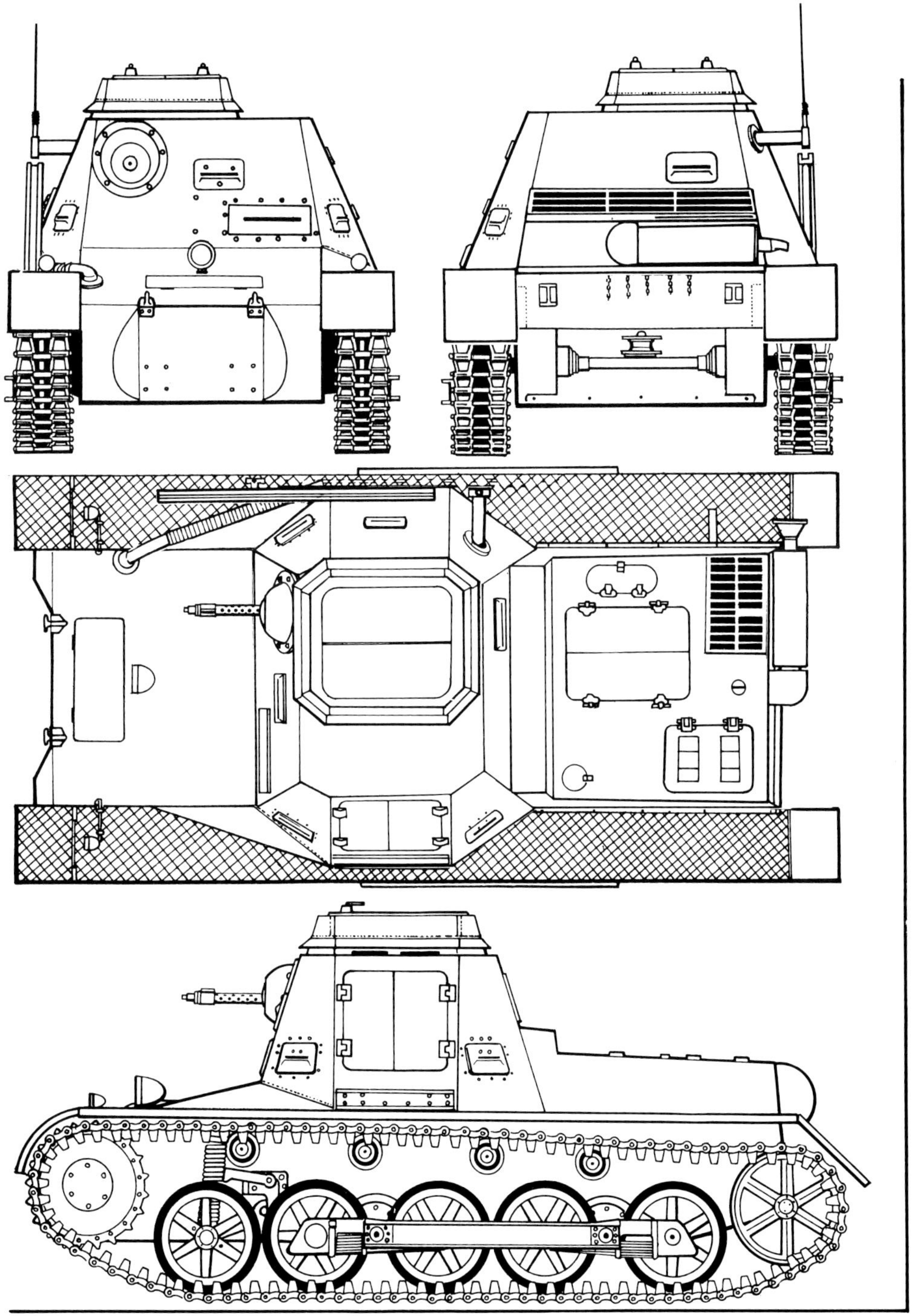

Panzerkampfwagen II Ausf. A, B, and C

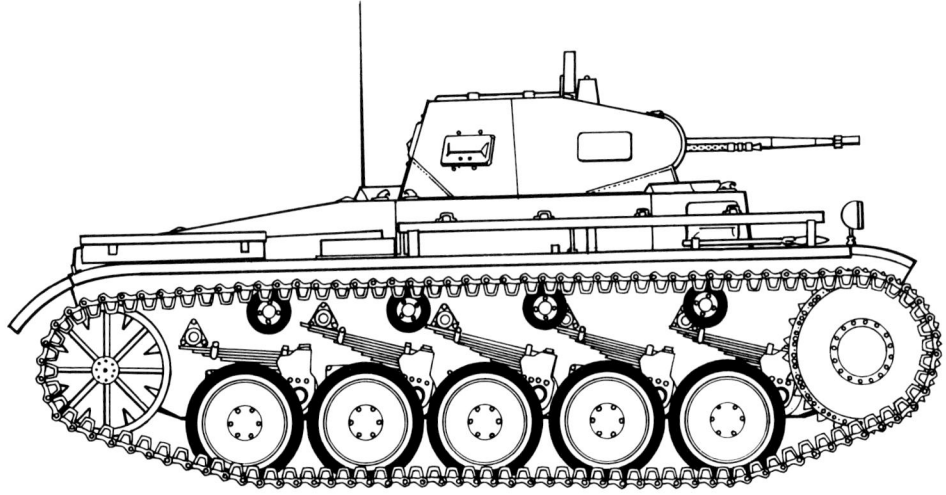

Development of Germany's main battle tanks, the Panzer III and IV, took longer than was originally planned when the long range development scheme was drawn up in the early 1930's. Many delays were caused by lack of materials and design problems. When the manufacturers of the Panzers III and IV announced that the vehicles would not be ready for production until 1938 or 1939, armored corp planners decided to go ahead with the production of a second type of interim vehicle; this one in the 10-ton range. Armament specifications called for a gun of 20mm caliber and an additional machine gun of rifle caliber. A 130 horsepower engine was chosen as the powerplant and contracts were let in 1934. By 1935 a number of manufacturers had produced prototype and test vehicles for evaluation by the Wehrmacht. The early versions of these new vehicles were designated **Panzerkampfwagen II (Sd.Kfz. 121)**, Ausf. a, b and c, and were put through a series of gruelling tests. The final contract was awarded to MAN and a number of pre-production vehicles were turned over to the Panzertruppe for further trials. Some of these trials took place in Spain where they were blooded against Soviet-built T-26 tanks armed with 45mm guns.

A number of changes were made to the Ausf. c model, such as the angled bow plate, as a result of lessons learned in earlier battles, but to all intents and purposes the later Panzer IIA, B and C were alike in all major respects. All three variants were powered by a Maybach six-cylinder liquid-cooled in-line engine that produced between 130 and 140 horsepower depending on the variant. The engine was fitted to a standard transmission with six forward and one reverse gear. The power shaft ran from the engine compartment through the fighting compartment to the transmission and final drive located in the front of the vehicle. Drive wheels were, of course, front mounted. The maximum road speed for these vehicles was 25 mph. Internal fuel capacity was 45 gallons and the maximum tactical

This *Panzer IIc* of 3. Panzer Division maneuvers up an embankment and over a pair of railroad tracks in France during winter maneuvers in January of 1941. The Panzer II was armed with a 20mm KwK 30 gun and a coaxial rifle-caliber 7.92 machine gun in the turret.

Panzerkampfwagen I Ausf. B of the 9. Panzer Division - Breda, Holland, May 1940.

Panzerkampfwagen I Ausf. A of the 21. Panzer Division - Libya, North Africa, March 1941.

Panzerkampfwagen II Ausf. A
of the 7. Panzer Division -
Kiev, Russia, August 1941.

Panzerkampfwagen 38(t) Ausf. H
of the 8. Panzer Division -
Dunkirchen (Dunkirk), April 1940.

range was 119 miles. The Panzer IIA, B, and C variants could cross trenches up to 68 inches in width and surmount vertical obstacles of up to 17 inches in height. Fording depth was set officially at 36", but at least one photograph in this section disputes that. Power to weight ratio was 14.7 horsepower per ton.

The **Pz.Kpfw. IIA, B,** and **C** tanks measured 15'9¼" in length, 7'5¾" in width, and 6'7½" in height. Although the weight of each variant differed only slightly, the average weight was 9.5 tons. Main armament of the tank was a single 20mm semi-automatic KwK 30 anti-tank gun. This gun had an effective range of some 700 yards and fired APCBC and tracer ammunition fitted in six-round magazines. A total of 30 magazines, or 180 rounds was the normal combat load. Secondary armament was a single 7.92mm machine gun mounted coaxially in the turret, next to the 20mm gun. The machine gun carried a combat load of 1425 rounds.

The hulls of the vehicles were of all-welded construction featuring heat treated steel armor of 30mm thickness at the bowplate, 31mm at the driver plate, 10mm on the side plates and 10mm on the rear plate. The turret of the vehicle was also of all-welded construction, utilizing armor of 30mm on the mantlet and frontplate, 16mm on the sides, 16mm in the rear, and 10mm on the top.

The Panzerkampfwagen IIA, B, and C variants were produced and issued to units between 1937 and 1940. Over 1000 of these vehicles participated in the Polish Campaign of 1939 with relatively light combat losses. When the battle for France started, there were still more than 900 Pz.Kpfw. II's in front line service. These vehicles proved to be quite effective as reconnaissance tanks, but did not measure up to the state of the art in terms of tank-to-tank action. They suffered from relatively light armor and were most definitely underarmed.

By 1940 it was clear that in order to retain the Panzer II in combat units, its armor would have to be thickened and its armament increased. These armor changes were later made to the vehicle and by 1941 a large number of Panzer II A, B, and C variants had been phased out or else retrofitted to new standards.

3. Panzer Division (early insignia)

A guard guides this *Panzer II, Ausführung* C over a platform of logs that has been erected over especially soft ground during the winter of 1940. The divisional symbol of the 3. Panzer Division — an inverted "Y" with two small dots to the side — can be seen on the right side of the driver's vision plate. This division remained in France until the spring of 1941 when it was re-equipped and sent to the East Front.

A *Panzer IIc* drives up a snowy hillside as infantry watch. This Pz. IIc bears the yellow divisional symbol of the 4. Panzer Division. In late 1940, this division lost one of its Panzer regiments, the 36th, which went to form the cadre of the 14. Panzer Division. The rest of the 4. Panzer went to Russia.

Drive sprocket and road wheel of Pz.Kpfw. II

A *Panzer IIc* of the 4. Panzer Division waits on the enfilade side of a hill. This vehicle bears a small plate on its rear decking which signifies the vehicles position in the company and batallion — a common practice for easy identification. Later in the war these numbers were transferred to the sides and rear of the turret.

March 16, 1939. A *Panzer II, Ausführung c* stands a quiet watch over a major traffic circle in Olmutz, Czechoslovakia. Elements of the German armed forces remained in Czechoslovakia to occupy the country after it was annexed in 1938. A major German force attacked north into Poland from Czechoslovakia at the beginning of the Polish campaign.

France, 1940. A *Panzer II* provides armor protection for a motorized patrol advancing toward a burning village. The vehicles at the front of the column are *Krupp Kfz 69* troop carriers which are followed by a motorcycle squad on *BMW R75* 'cycles.

Black Panzer 'Kappi' NCO (Side cap with earphone)

A *Panzer IIB* negotiates a steep embankment. The *Pz.Kw.IIc* was the final development of the early series and became the first major production type. First produced in 1937, over 2000 of the later Ausf. A, B and C types were built. These later versions had the angled bowplate where earlier versions carried the rounded bowplate.

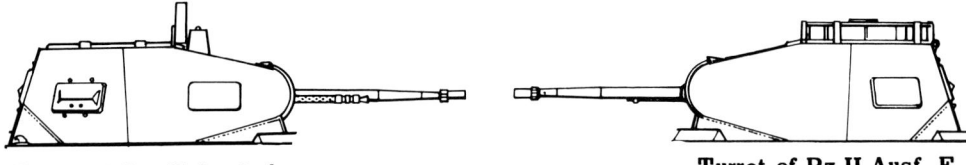

Turret of Pz. II Ausf. A **Turret of Pz II Ausf. F**

The *Panzer II Ausf. A* was externally distinguishable from the earlier Ausf. c by the angled nose armor plate. The armor was increased, raising the combat weight to 9.5 tons. The commander's hatch is a two piece square arrangement with the observation periscope mounted in front.

A *Pz. IIA* and *Ausf. c* move slowly along a cobblestoned street in the heart of Warsaw during the last days of September 1939. The formation marking on the turret of the nearest vehicle is "R03", indicative of a regimental staff vehicle. The whitewashed cross on the turret was common to most German vehicles operating during the Polish campaign and later became the basis from which the Germans applied their national insignia to their armored vehicles.

This *Panzer IIA* was knocked out during the hard fighting in Warsaw during the closing days of the campaign. The tank has obviously lost a tread but a closer look between the first and second road wheels shows that the axle and leaf spring suspension have been thoroughly destroyed by either a land mine or some explosive device placed under the tank. The MG mount on the turret top was an improvision only temporarily used during the Polish campaign.

Adolf Hitler and a number of commanders take the salute from German armored formations of Panzer II's as they pass by the reviewing platform during a victory parade in Warsaw, Poland, at the end of the hostilities there. The vehicle commanders are in the turrets while the third members of the tank crews sit at attention on the fenders with their feet in the crew entry hatches. Of the 2574 Panzers participating in this campaign 955 were Panzer II's.

(Above left) A *Panzer IIc* of an unidentified unit participates in a victory parade through the streets of the units' home town in Germany during the spring of 1940. An honor guard of Panzer Korps troops armed with rifles stand at parade rest on the sidewalk as the vehicles pass by the crowd.

Operation "Weserübung" the invasion of Norway in April 1940. *Panzer II Ausf.* c and a *Panzer IB* of the 4. Panzer Division on patrol outside Trontheim.

NORWAY
April 9, 1940

OPERATION "WESERÜBUNG"

A *Panzer IIc* and a group of infantrymen patrol this road outside of Oslo, Norway. The Panzer IIC version can be recognized by its rounded bowplate and the absence of a commander's cupola on the top of the turret.

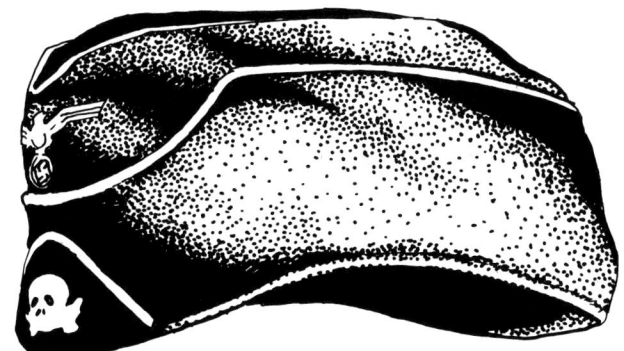

Black Panzer-Feldmutze (Officer)

This *Panzer II* carries a pair of infantrymen on its rear decking as an extra protective measure against guerrillas or partisans that may be hiding around this Norwegian railroad bridge or inside the tunnel ahead. As the war progressed guerrilla activities became a very real thorn in the side of the German war machine.

During a break in action, the crew of this *Panzer II* picks up a supply of machine gun ammunition in the saddle drums on the fender of the vehicle and at the same time finds time to have a hot meal of stew and black bread.

(Below right) This *Pz.Kpfw. II Ausf A* of the 6. Panzer Division slowly negotiates a pontoon bridge over a French river that has been erected by German combat engineers. Note the logs on the right side of the vehicle's rear decking. These were used to extricate the vehicle from boggy or muddy terrain by placing them in front of the treads of the tank.

A *Panzer II Ausf. A* of the 4. Panzer Division throws back a spray of mud as she hustles along this French forest road during a frosty May morning just after the invasion began. The tank commander is wearing a field gray great coat since no black ones were issued. Note that this vehicle is not equipped with a commander's cupola, but has a simple rectangular hatch instead.

An engineer assists in filling a muddy embankment with dry earth to aid the traction of the *Panzer IIc* that is attempting to negotiate it. This vehicle has just forded a river and its weight, plus the weight of vehicles before it has made the bank too soft for armor to cross. The Panzer II is from the 1. Panzer Division.

A *Panzer II Ausf. B* of the 3. Panzer Division is loaded on a German freighter to be shipped to North Africa. The Panzers of the 5. Regiment 3. Pz. Div. were the first German tanks to arrive in Africa, February 1941.

(Below right) The *Panzer IIC,* left, and *Ausf. B,* second from the left, are vehicles of the 5. Light Division, formed from the nucleus of the 5. Panzer Regiment. The 5. Light Division served in North Africa until it was redesignated the 21. Panzer Division.

Panzer II Ausf. C with antennas raised on a communications trial. The Ausf. C differs externally from the Ausf. B (the second vehicle) by the conical idler wheel, the muffler arrangement and the absence of the smoke discharger.

Maintenance units closely followed the advancing Panzers with all necessary equipment to conduct major repairs immediately. The mechanic on the left is jacking up the front end of a *Panzer IIIF* while the one on the right is assisting with a block and tackle that has been attached to a cable slung between two trees. A Panzer IIC of the 4. Panzer Division awaits attention in the foreground.

(Above left) Old antagonists meet again. A *Panzer II* moves past an abandoned Soviet T-26C light tank mounting a 45mm gun in its turret. Russia was not the first place that T-26's and Panzer II's met in combat, both types received their baptisms of fire in the Spanish Civil War between 1937 and 1939.

The relative fordability of the Panzer II is obvious here as one crosses a river with the waves lapping at the open driver's visor and the engine top decking. It appears that the only person inside the tank is the driver. The other two crewmembers (wearing black caps) and an infantryman hang onto the superstructure and turret sides as the Panzer II moves through the water.

Panzerkampfwagen IIF (Sd.Kfz. 121)

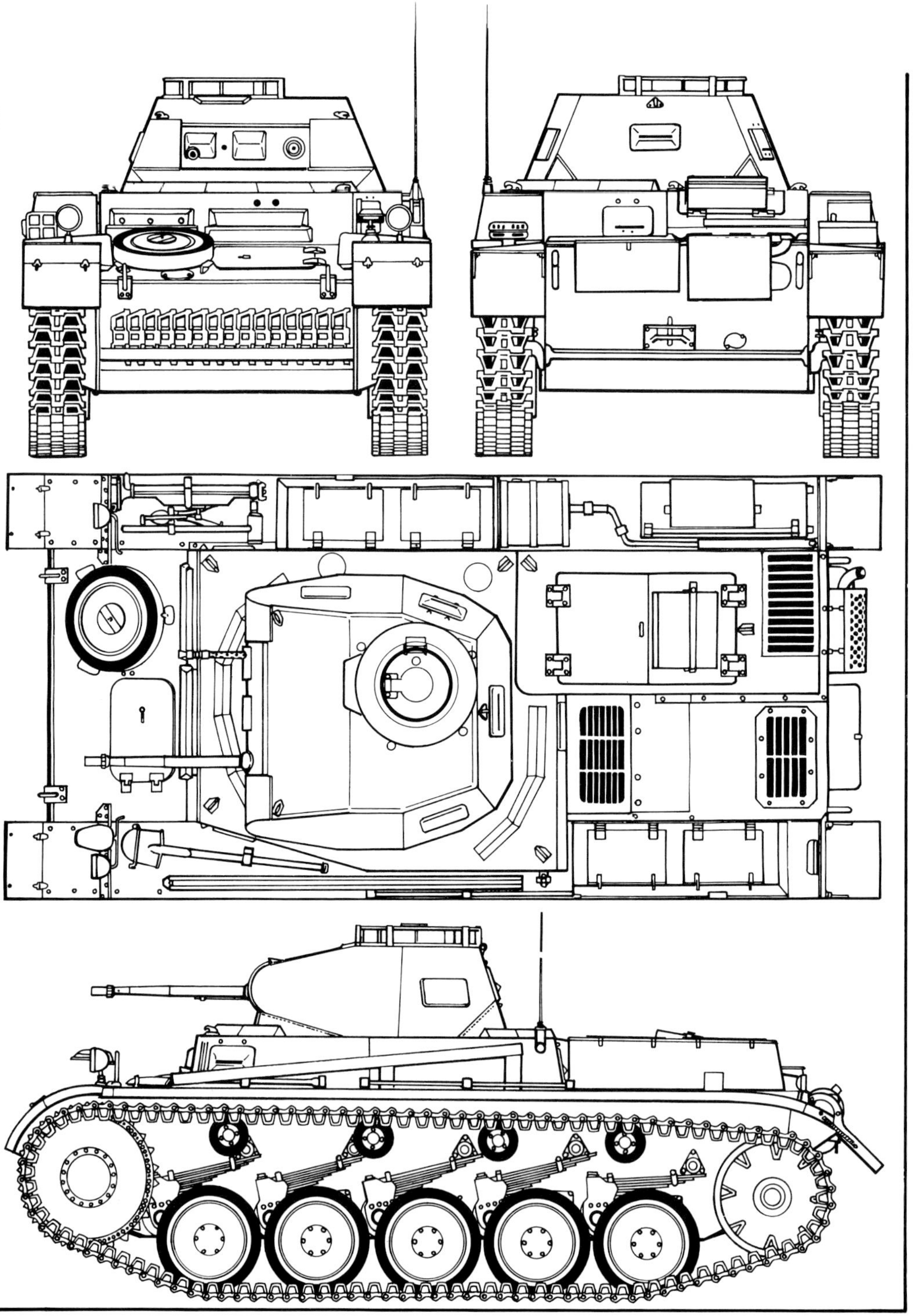

TECHNICAL DATA

Manufacturer	MAN, Wegmann, Henschel, Miag
Production Year	1940 - 1943
No. Built	625 vehicles
Crew	3 men
Weight	9.5 tons (9500 kg)
Length	15'9¼"
Width	7'5¾"
Height	6'7½"
Engine	6 cyl. water cooled Maybach HL 62 TRM
Horsepower	140 hp/2600 r.p.m.
Transmission	6 forward, 1 reverse
Steering	gearbox epicyclic steering
Track width	300 mm
Clearance	340 mm
Armor	Front 30/35 mm, side 14,5mm, rear 20mm
Armament	1 x 20 mm KwK 38 L/55, 1 x MG 34
Ammunition	180 rds. 20 mm, 2550 rds. 7.92 mm
Fuel	2 tanks 170 ltr. (appr. 43 Imp. gal.)
Consumption	Road 110 ltr., cross country 170 ltr. (100 km)
Range	Road 150 km., cross country 100 km
Top speed	40 km/h (25 m.p.h.)

Panzerkampfwagen II F

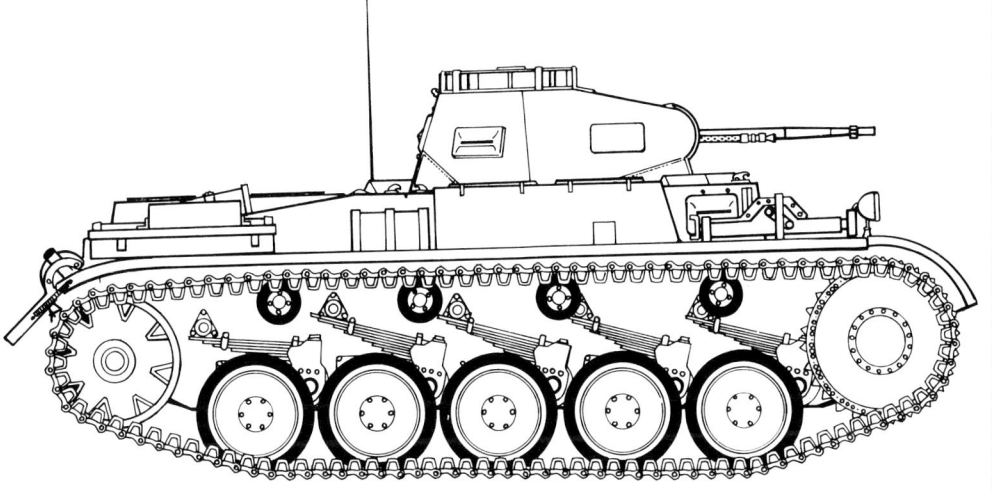

The **Panzer IIF** was the first of a "new breed" on the old chassis of the earlier Panzer II variants. It first appeared in late 1940. The major structural change to the vehicle was the addition of more armor, the bowplate armor on the chassis was increased to 36mm, the driver plate armor was thickened to 31mm and the rest of the chassis armor was increased to 20mm. The armor on the turret remained the same as that for the A, B, and C variants, except for the mantlet and frontplate, which was increased to 32mm. All of this additional armor increased the vehicles' weight to over ten tons which put a severe strain on the 140 horsepower engine.

A new main gun, the 20mm KwK 38, was fitted in place of the older gun. The KwK 38 fired the same round as the KwK 30, but the slight increase in barrel length added more velocity to the 20mm rounds, making the gun more effective. The single rifle caliber MG remained as secondary armament and the machine gun ammunition was standardized at 2550 rounds.

Even though changes were made to the vehicles' armor, powerplant, and main armament, the **Panzerkampfwagen IIF,** did not prove to be much better of a vehicle than the earlier series. They were defeated by other comparatively weighted tanks, simply because the enemy vehicles carried larger main armament. The introduction of the shaped charge and its use against the Panzer II was the main reason for increasing the vehicles' armor, but in the long run, this modification gave the **Sd.Kfz. 121** only a few more months of life as a battle tank. By 1942 production of the tank version of this vehicle had ceased and more and more chassis were being converted or modified into special purpose vehicles. It must be remembered, though, that in the years of the Wehrmacht's greatest victories, the Panzer II made up the majority of the Panzertruppe vehicles and in the hands of a good crew, this light Panzer performed well.

An armored infantry unit of the "Grossdeutschland" division pauses next to a pond somewhere in Russia. A *Sd.Kfz. 10* light personnel carrier leads the column while *Sd.Kfz. 251/1* medium armored personnel carriers make up the rest of the column. The third vehicle of the column is a *Krupp "Protze" Kfz. 69* truck pulling a 20mm flak gun on a trailer. The Panzer II in the foreground is a model F carrying its own extra supply of gasoline in 20 liter "jerricans".

With increased armor plating and additional stowage boxes, the *Panzer II Ausf. F* is readily identified by the Pz. III type driver's visor. The dummy visor to the left has no function other than to increase the armor protection. This advance unit of the Panzer Division "Grossdeutschland" is in direct radio contact with the Fieseler "Storch" observation plane, keeping a close surveillance on the retreating enemy, Russia, August 1941.

(Below left) Panzers and trucks of the "Grossdeutschland" division wait in an assembly area and watch as dive bombers strike Russian targets in the distance. The *Panzer IIF* in the foreground has a flag attached to its engine cover as a means of identification when viewed from the air. The vehicle directly in front of the tank is a *Horch Kfz. 15* medium passenger car. To the immediate right of the tank is a *Horch Kfz. 17* radio van and in front of it is a second Kfz. 15 passenger car.

A Panzer IIF of a Stabs-kompanie (headquarters unit) on its way to the rear passes a not-too-motorized supply column carrying supplies forward. Many people have the mistaken idea that Germany's army was almost all motorized, this is of course not the case. Hundreds of thousands of draft animals were in use and this picture is closer to reality than long lines of vehicles.

A *Pz.Kw. IIB* brings up the rear of a column of Panzers on this dusty road in the central sector of the East Front during the summer of 1941. The tank carries a flag on her rear deck for aerial identification purposes. The vastness of the Russian terrain put hard strains on the Panzertruppe and a shortage of fuel and spare parts hampered the exploitation of the rapid advances during the summer of 1941.

(Below left) During the first four months of the Russian campaign the Germans fought over the type of terrain shown in this photo. *Panzer IIF* tanks accompany infantry over the steppe. In the background an infantry unit has set up a command post and erected a field radio set with a two meter antenna. These vehicles are painted overall dark sand, and are taking part in the encirclement of Smolensk.

As light artillery strikes a Russian village ahead, an armored column waits to move up. The column is made up of light armored personnel carriers, medium armored personnel carriers, a communication vehicle on the medium armored personnel carrier chassis, a *Panzer II* tank in the foreground and *Panzer III* tanks to its right.

A *Panzer IIF* has broken through Soviet lines and taken three Soviet prisoners. The three prisoners will be sent to the rear to be interrogated by military police and military intelligence personnel. Note the open padded commander escape hatch.

Idler wheel of Pz. II Ausf. c, A, B, C

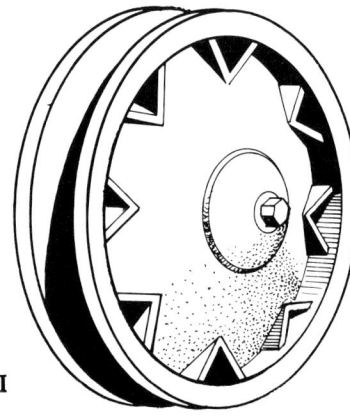

Idler wheel of Pz. II Ausf. F

The crew of a tired *Panzer IIF* loaded down with gear and loot on its rear deck gets a good natured ribbing from the crews of *Marder II* self-propelled guns in the background. The Marder II was built on the chassis of the Pz.Kw. II and mounted the highly effective 75mm Pak 40/2 anti-tank gun.

Panzerkampfwagen 35(t)

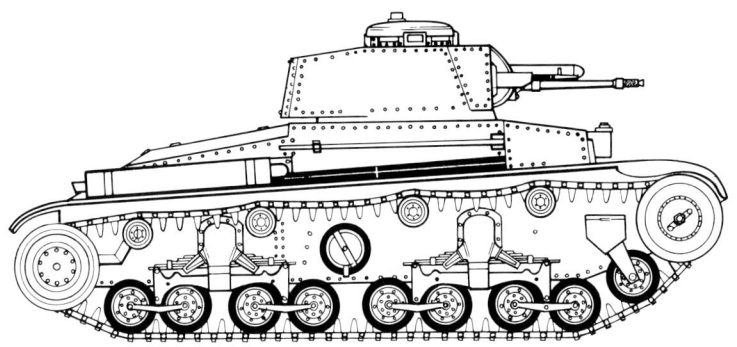

In 1935, the Skoda machine works in Czechoslovakia produced a new armored fighting vehicle for the army, weighing 11 tons, the vehicle was designated **Skoda LTM35** and featured a number of very advanced construction and subassembly concepts that were adopted only later by many other manufacturers of armored vehicles. Some of these advanced features included the installation of the drive sprockets at the rear of the vehicle, rather than the front. This was done to keep the fighting compartment free of the drive shaft or drive mechanism. The power train ran almost directly from the engine to the drive sprockets, passing only through the transmission and final reduction gears. Power assisted brakes, transmission and steering were installed, using compressed air as the assistant force. These were innovations that went far toward reducing the physical wear and tear on the driver. An additional feature was the suspension system that distributed the weight of the vehicle evenly on all of the bogie wheels. This feature increased the life of the tracks to an average of 4000 miles when other vehicles of that era were averaging 1000 miles of track life.

The LTM 35 tanks first reached Czechoslovakian units in 1937. They were used specifically in the infantry support or infantry accompaniment role. Main armament of the LTM 35 was a 37mm Skoda A-3 tank gun with not only a high rate of fire, but high muzzle velocity and fine ballistics with armor-piercing shot. Secondary armament was a pair of rifle caliber machine guns; one mounted in the turret, the other in the bowplate.

The vehicle was powered by a 6-cylinder in-line Skoda T-11 engine that produced 120 horsepower at 1800 rpm. Although the power to weight ratio was only a mediocre 10.3 horsepower per ton, this was somewhat bettered by the installation of a 12 speed gearbox featuring 6 forward and 6 reverse gears. Top speed was 21 mph and internal fuel capacity was 41 gallons, giving the vehicle a tactical range of 119 miles.

The crew of the vehicle consisted of four men; the driver, bow machine gunner, gunner for the main armament, and the tank commander. When Germany absorbed Czechoslovakia into the Reich in March 1939, she defeated one of the world's best equipped armies without firing a single shot. The Czech army was simply incorporated into the Wehrmacht. The Czech LTM 35 was redesignated **Panzerkampfwagen 35(t)** and entire units of these vehicles became parts of new Panzer divisions.

These Czech-built tanks took part in the Polish Campaign in small numbers and due to their robust construction, very few were lost due to mechanical breakdowns. One major weak point noted during the Polish Campaign was the construction techniques used to build the chassis, hull and turret. Despite all of her other advanced features, the Panzerkampfwagen 35(t) was held together by rivets, a technique that was behind the times in comparison to the German all-welded technique.

Since production of these vehicles continued after Czechoslovakia was absorbed into the Reich, a comparatively large number of Panzer 35(t) vehicles were in use when France was invaded during 1940. These tanks served the Germans well and enabled the Wehrmacht to field more Panzer divisions than German industry could have supplied by itself.

When Germany invaded the Soviet Union in 1941, large numbers of the Panzer 35(t) were on hand, serving the Germans as well as the Hungarians, Rumanians, and Italians. Once again their robust construction allowed these vehicles to play a meaningful role in certain areas during the early months of the invasion. During the winter of 1941-42, the coldest reported in the Soviet Union in more than 20 years, the German armies ground to a standstill on the East Front. Lack of supplies, partisan activities and extremely low temperatures created many problems for the Wehrmacht. The Panzer 35(t) suffered far more than any other German tank because of her compressed air systems which simply froze solid. After that first deadly winter many Panzer 35(t)'s had their compressed air systems removed and mechanical systems installed in their places.

As with many other obsolete or obsolescent tracked vehicles in service with the Wehrmacht, the **Panzerkampfwagen 35(t)** chassis were used for other purposes, such as mortar carriers, prime movers and supply vehicles long after their use as battle tanks had been replaced by more modern vehicles.

This *Panzer 35(t)* was knocked out during the Polish campaign by running over a land mine and blowing off its tread. It is conceivable that the blast of the mine knocked some rivets loose from the superstructure, causing them to fly around the fighting compartment, killing or injuring members of the crew.

(Above right) A Czechoslovakian built *Panzer 35(t)* of the 6. Panzer Division stands guard in a French forest. The Panzer 35(t) made up the bulk of the armor in the 6. Panzer Division when it participated in the French campaign of 1940. It was armed with a 37mm cannon and a pair of rifle-caliber machine guns.

(Below right) Approximately one hundred *Panzer 35(t)*s participated in the French Campaign. Not only the 6. Panzer Division, as erroneously stated in a number of publications, but also the 3. Panzer Division were issued the Pz. 35(t).

This interesting view shows the crew of this *Panzer 35(t)* preparing their vehicle and their personal gear for an inspection. Some members of the crew have circled the small arms hits their vehicle has taken on the turret with white paint.

The *Panzer 35(t)* was fitted with a Skoda (Czech-built) A-3 37mm gun, characterized by the large recoil mechanism mounted over the barrel of the gun. The 7.92mm machine guns on the bow and turret were manufactured at the Brno small arms plant, one of the world's finest manufacturers of automatic weapons.

(Below left) This Czech *Panzer 35(t)* could climb a gradient of 29 degrees, cross a trench of 6.5 ft. and wade a creek up to a depth of 2.6 feet. Note that the engine air intakes on the rear decking have been covered by specially made heavy duty canvas covers on to which a flag has been sewed for air recognition purposes. The cold Russian weather played havoc with the compressed air assisted gear change and brakes in these vehicles.

A column of *Pz.Kw. 35(t)* tanks of the 14. Panzer Division patrols a dirt road somewhere in the northern sector of the Russian Front during the autumn of 1941. Note that each vehicle carries a special rack on its rear deck onto which six 20-liter gasoline cans have been attached.

Panzerkampfwagen 35(t)

TECHNICAL DATA

Manufacturer	Skoda
Production Year	1935 - 1937
No. Built	300 vehicles
Crew	4 men
Weight	10.5 tons (10500 kg)
Length	14'8"
Width	7'
Height	7'2"
Engine	6 cyl. water cooled Skoda T-11
Horsepower	120 hp/1800 r.p.m.
Transmission	6 forward, 6 reverse
Steering	clutch and brake
Track width	320 mm
Clearance	350 mm
Armor	Front 25 mm, side 16mm, rear 12 mm
Armament	1 x Skoda 37 mm L/40, 2 x MG type 37
Ammunition	90 rds. 37 mm, 2550 rds. 7.92 mm.
Fuel	153 ltr. (appr. 41 Imp. gal.)
Consumption	Road 80 ltr., cross country 120 ltr. (100 km)
Range	Road 190 km., cross country 120 km.
Top speed	34 km/h (21 m.p.h.)

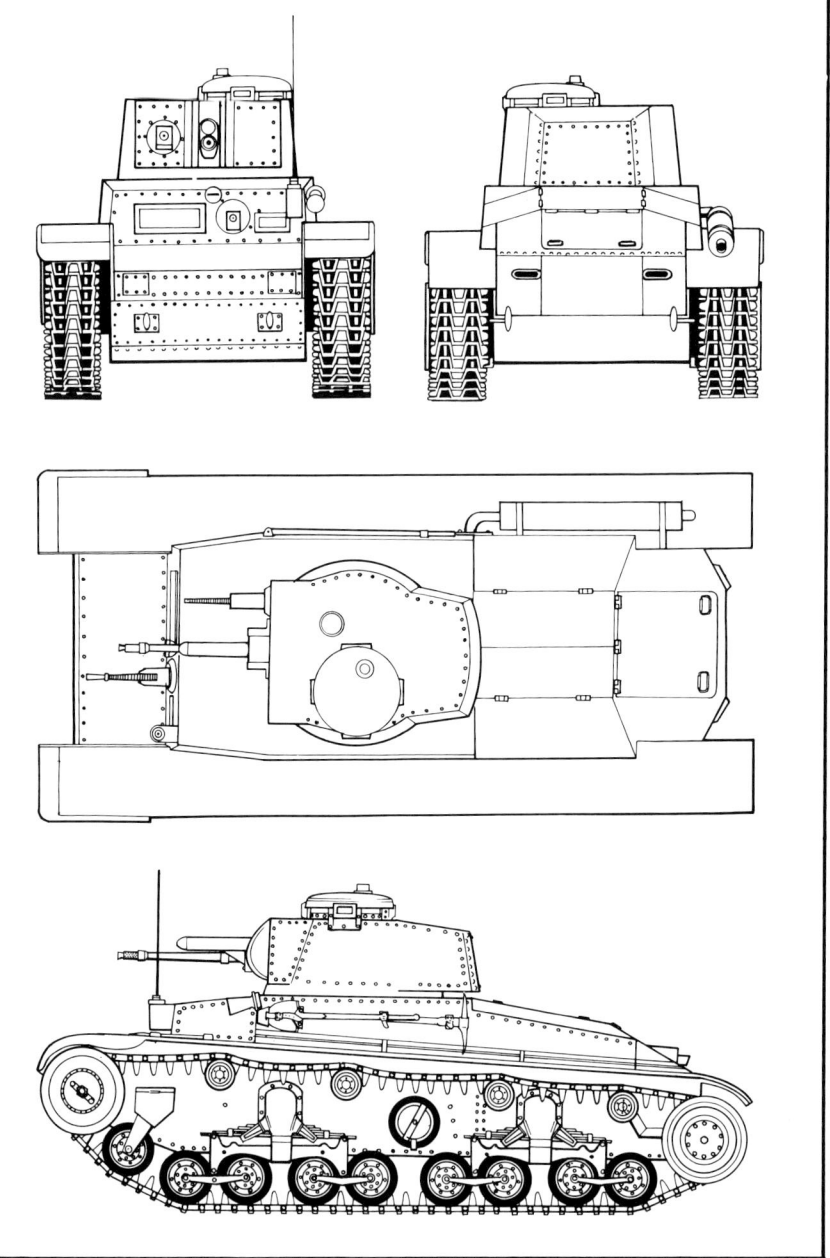

Panzerkampfwagen 38 (t)

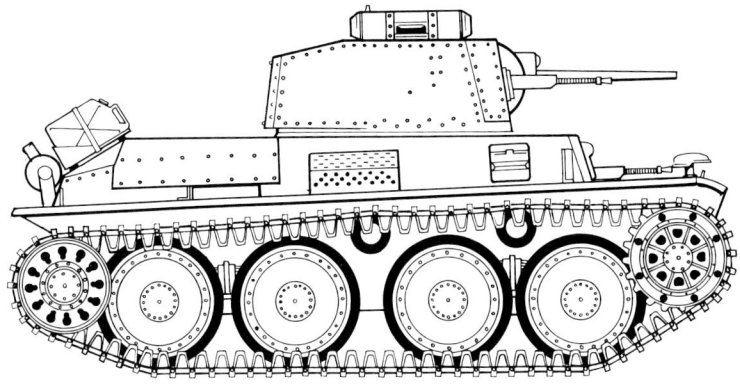

Perhaps no tank of foreign origin was as important to the Panzertruppe as the Czech-built **Panzer 38**(t). This vehicle formed the basis from which a large number of special purpose variants were developed to give long and useful service to the Germans in especially large numbers throughout the war.

Not only was the **LT-38** (its Czech designation) very useful to the Germans, it was also one of the most successful products of Czechoslovakia's armament industry before the Second World War.

The **Panzerkampfwagen 38**(t) was a robust vehicle of all riveted construction and its design set a precedent for future armored vehicle development. The vehicle weighed 10.5 tons when fitted for combat, was 16 feet long, seven feet high and 7 feet wide. She was powered by a Praga EPA 6-cylinder 473 cubic inch engine that produced 125 horsepower at 2200 rpm. The transmission was standard with five forward and one reverse gear. Internal fuel capacity was 49 Imp. Gal., enough to give the tank a range of 120 miles. Top speed of the vehicle was 25 mph.

The four large road wheels on either side of the chassis gave the Panzer 38(t) the outward appearance of a Christie-type suspension, but in reality each pair of axles was attached to the ends of a horizontal leaf spring mounted to a common crossmember which distributed the weight of the vehicle on an equal basis to each road wheel.

The Panzer 38(t) was armed with a Skoda A-3, 37mm L40 and a pair of 7.92mm machine guns; one in the bow and the other in the turret. Ammunition stowage for the main gun was limited to 90 rounds, while the machine guns had a load of 2700 rounds.

Production of the Panzer 38(t) continued after Germany annexed Czechoslovakia in 1939. Around 40 vehicles a month were produced between 1939 and 1942. These vehicles were well liked by the crews that operated them and before the Battle of France in 1940, almost two entire divisions of **Panzer 38(t)'s** were absorbed into the strength of the Panzer corps. By the beginning of the Soviet campaign in 1941, the strength of the Panzer 38(t) had grown in numbers to almost 800 vehicles. This was almost one quarter of Germany's entire tank strength.

As with so many other vehicles, the Soviet campaign and its rigors brought an end to the use of the **Panzerkampfwagen 38**(t) as a main battle tank. Her comparatively weak main armament proved incapable of defeating any but the lightest of Soviet tanks and armored cars.

Even though the Soviet campaign spelled an end to the Panzer 38(t) use as a tank, it brought forth a new career in the form of a large number of special purpose vehicles and construction of the chassis continued until May of 1944.

A *BMW R75* **motorcycle with red cross markings on the sidecar, is leading** *Panzer 38(t)s* **and** *Panzer IIA's* **of the 7. Panzer Division on a dusty Russian road. Summer 1941.**

Panzer 38(t) tanks of the 16. Panzer Division follow a dusty road somewhere in the southern sector of the East Front. The 16. Panzer Division was ultimately attached to Von Paulus' Sixth Army where it fought heroically during the battle for Stalingrad. There it was decimated and the survivors fell into Soviet hands. A new 16. Panzer Division was later formed and fought in Italy.

6. Pz. Div.   7. Pz. Div.   8. Pz. Div.

(Below right) The *Panzer 38(t)* was an extremely robust vehicle. Built by the Ceskomoravska Kolben Danek works of Prague in Czechoslovakia, these vehicles were highly prized by the Germans who equipped two full armored divisions with them for the battle of France. This Pz.Kw. 38(t) operating in Russia bears the Roman numeral "III" of a 3rd Battalion staff vehicle on her turret sides.

The Smolensk suburbs are reached! A *Pz. 38(t)* is supporting the infantry in clearing a barricade on a railroad crossing. Over 750 Pz. 38(t)s served with the 7. and 8. Pz. Div. during their first year in Russia.

Rear view of the *Panzer 38(t) Model E* with Russian volunteers training in France. The round maintenance hatch allowed easy accessibility to the 6 cyl. Skoka engine.

(Above right) The Hungarian Army received a number of the *Pz. 38(t)*. This one was disabled by a land mine. The turret MG is blown out by the internal explosion and the hull MG was removed and covered by a round plate indicating that the vehicle was a commander's model.

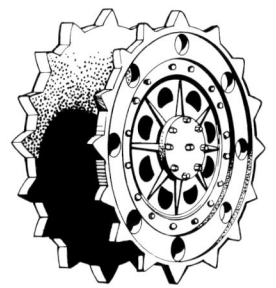

Drive wheel of Pz. 38(t)H

A *Panzer 38(t)* provides protection while all-important fuel is unloaded from railway cars and a fueling point is set up. This photograph was taken in the Smolensk area of the Soviet Union on October 4th, 1941.

49

Panzerkampfwagen 38(t)

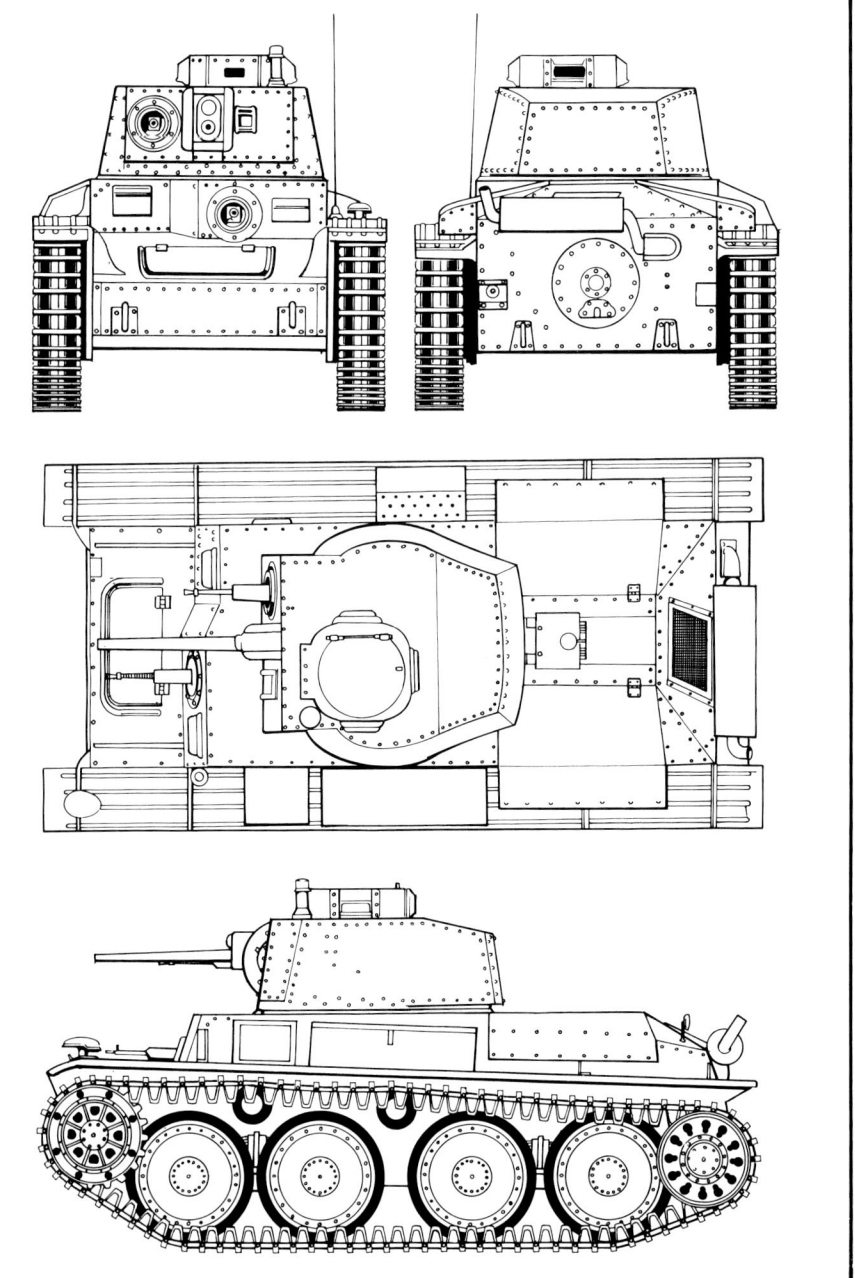

Manufacturer	Praga
Production Year	1937 - 1942
No. Built	1500
Crew	4 men
Weight	10.5 tons (10500 kg)
Length	16'
Width	7'
Height	7'
Engine	6 cyl. water cooled Praga EPA
Horsepower	125 hp/2200 r.p.m.
Transmission	5 forward, 1 reverse
Steering	clutch and brake
Track width	293 mm
Clearance	400 mm
Armor	Front 25 mm, side 15 mm, rear 12 mm
Armament	1 x Skoda A3 37 mm L/40, 2 x MG type 37
Ammunition	90 rds. 37 mm, 2700 rds. 7.92 mm
Fuel	218 ltr. (appr. 49 Imp. gal.)
Consumption	Road 90 ltr., cross country 135 ltr. (100 km.)
Range	Road 250 km., cross country 160 km.
Top speed	42 km/h (25 m.p.h.)